I0816546

SPY GUIDE

SPY EVASION

ELSIE OLSON

Abdo & Daughters
MIDDLE GRADE NONFICTION

An imprint of Abdo Publishing
abdobooks.com

ABDOBOOKS.COM

Published by Abdo Publishing, a division of ABDO, PO Box 398166, Minneapolis, Minnesota 55439.

Printed in the United States of America, North Mankato, Minnesota
052024
092024

Design: Kelly Doudna, Mighty Media, Inc.
Production: Mighty Media, Inc.
Editor: Katherine Chu
Cover Photographs: Flickr, Wikimedia Commons

Interior Photographs: Adobe Stock, pp. 58–59; Alamy Photo, pp. 32, 42; AP Images, pp. 37, 50, 61 (top right); Flickr, pp. 18, 38, 44; Getty Images, pp. 40–41; iStockphoto, pp. 4–5, 6, 17, 19, 55; Library of Congress, pp. 28, 30–31, 60 (top, bottom right); Shutterstock Images, pp. 1, 12–13, 14, 20, 35, 36, 39, 52–53, 56; Wikimedia Commons, pp. 8, 9, 10, 16, 21, 22–23, 25, 26, 34, 46–47, 48, 51, 54, 60 (bottom left), 61 (top left, top middle, bottom left, bottom middle, bottom right)

Design Elements: Adobe Stock

Library of Congress Control Number: 2023949603

Publisher's Cataloging-in-Publication Data
Names: Olson, Elsie, author.
Title: Spy evasion / by Elsie Olson
Description: Minneapolis, Minnesota : Abdo Publishing, 2025 | Series: Spy guide | Includes online resources and index.
Identifiers: ISBN 9781098293154 (lib. bdg.) | ISBN 9798384912422 (ebook)
Subjects: LCSH: Escapes--Juvenile literature. | Infiltration (Military science)--Juvenile literature. | Gadgets--Juvenile literature. | Espionage--Juvenile literature. | Spies--Juvenile literature.
Classification: DDC 327.12--dc23

CONTENTS

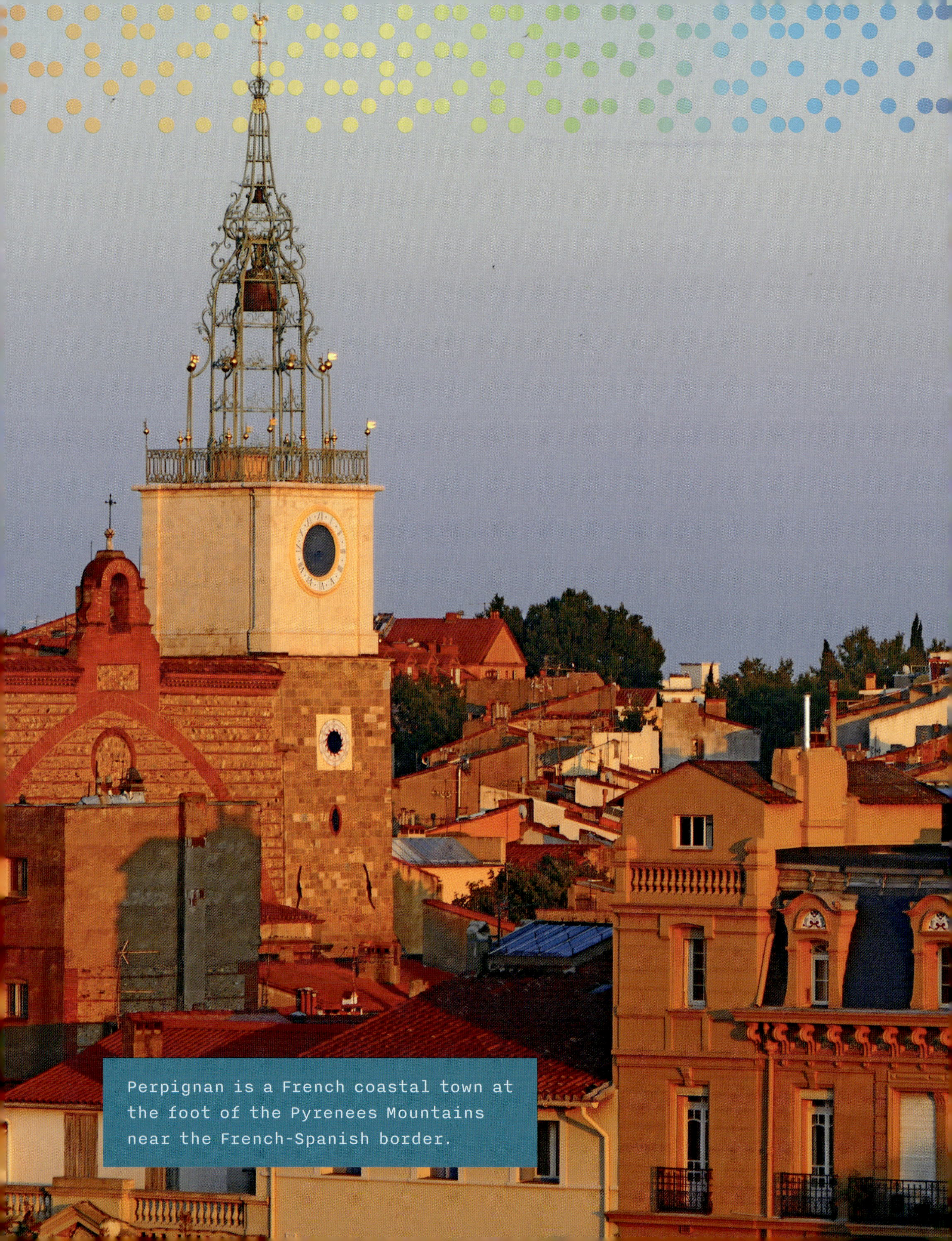

Perpignan is a French coastal town at the foot of the Pyrenees Mountains near the French-Spanish border.

CHAPTER 1

THE WHITE MOUSE ESCAPES AGAIN

It's 1943 and a train is traveling across France from Toulouse to Perpignan. Suddenly, a railway official rushes through the cars, warning passengers that Nazi guards are searching the train for French Resistance fighters.

World War II has been ongoing, and France has spent the last three years under German Nazi occupation. Throughout this time, a group of fighters, spies, and saboteurs known as the French Resistance has done its best to fight back against the Nazis. They are so effective that Germany has ordered the Gestapo, or Nazi police, to hunt them down.

A DARING ESCAPE

As the railway official warns the passengers, one woman quickly rises from her seat. She is Nancy Wake, a Resistance fighter and spy, nicknamed "the White Mouse" by the Gestapo.

To get to Spain, Wake needed to cross the Pyrenees Mountains.

With a five-million-franc bounty on her head, she is at the top of the Gestapo's most-wanted list. So it's vital she reach Spain, a country that has remained neutral during the war. From there, she can travel to an Allied country, such as England, and continue fighting the Germans.

Wake has already had many close calls with the Germans. During a previous escape attempt, Nazi police arrested Wake, beating and questioning her for four days. But she refused to reveal any information about her identity or the Resistance. Eventually they released Wake, thanks to Albert Guérisse, the head of the Pat O'Leary Line, a French Resistance group that helped captured Allied soldiers escape France.

Guérisse posed as a French officer working for German police. He claimed Wake was his girlfriend who was afraid of her husband learning about their affair. The Germans believed him and let Wake go.

Wake will not be caught again. She climbs through a window and jumps from the moving train, leaving her belongings and identity cards behind. She takes off running, the sound of gunfire echoing behind her. Though she must wait another day to get to Spain, the White Mouse has escaped again.

AN UNLIKELY SPY

Nancy Grace Augusta Wake was born in New Zealand and grew up in Sydney, Australia. After inheriting money from an aunt at age 16, she moved to London, England, where she started working as a journalist.

Wake eventually moved to Paris, France. There, she met and married wealthy French businessman Henri Fiocca, and they settled in Marseille, France. When the Nazis occupied France in 1940, Wake and Fiocca were disturbed by their cruel treatment of Jewish people. So they joined the O'Leary Line French Resistance group.

As a member of the O'Leary Line, Wake drove an ambulance, helping refugees escape France and delivering top-secret messages within the Resistance network. Using her position as a wealthy socialite, she also convinced guards to give her access to restricted information and areas.

At checkpoints, Nazi officers were so charmed by Wake that they didn't bother to search her.

By 1943, the Nazis had become suspicious of Wake's activities. France was no longer safe for her. One day, Wake told Fiocca she was going shopping, kissed him goodbye, and left for Spain. It took Wake six attempts to get to Spain and then England safely. Unfortunately, after her escape, the Gestapo arrested and executed Fiocca for refusing to reveal Wake's location.

THE SOE

When Wake arrived in England in June 1943, she kept fighting the Germans. At the time, most military and intelligence operations believed women were unfit for espionage and combat, but one British intelligence group felt differently.

In 1940, England had set up an elite force of guerrilla fighters, saboteurs, and spies called the Special Operations Executive (SOE).

The SOE worked behind enemy lines to gather secret information, or intelligence, and disrupt German operations. In the words of British prime minister Winston Churchill, the SOE's mission was to "set Europe ablaze."

It didn't take long for SOE leaders to value female agents. Women were rarely searched at checkpoints, so they could carry messages through enemy territory. And they were just as smart, strong, and capable as male officers. Wake joined 39 female spies who would help the Resistance in France.

Wake spent eight months training in espionage tactics, including resisting interrogation and guerrilla warfare. She learned how to shoot a gun and set up explosives. She also learned hand-to-hand combat and wilderness survival. Wake excelled at her training, becoming a highly skilled fighter.

After World War II, Wake was awarded multiple medals and honors. These included the US Medal of Freedom, the *Médaille de la Résistance*, and the *Croix de Guerre*.

During World War II, 39 of 470 SOE agents were female. Some of these agents included (*clockwise from top left*) Odette Sansom, Violette Szabo, Yvonne Cormeau, and Noor Inayat Khan.

THE WORK BEGINS

In 1944, Wake parachuted into Auvergne, France, beginning her SOE work. She trained French fighters, organized weapons and supplies deliveries, and transported messages. At one point, fearing capture by the Germans, Wake's radio operator destroyed their communication code books. This meant Wake could no longer contact London. Wake biked more than 300 miles (500 km) in three days to reestablish contact, since she knew she had a better chance of getting through the checkpoints along the route. This journey became one of Wake's proudest moments during the war.

After the war, Wake lived the rest of her life in Australia and England. She died in 2011 at age 98. At her request, Wake's ashes were scattered over the hills of France, where she had spent what she considered the most important years of her life. She once said, "It's all been so exciting … and then it all fizzled out. I had a very happy war." Wake is remembered as a gifted spy who helped the Allies win World War II with her espionage skills.

A diplomat at a foreign embassy could be used as an official cover. Spies operating under official cover use their real identities and are protected by their government if caught.

CHAPTER 2

ESPIONAGE 101

ESPIONAGE IS THE ART OF STEALING SECRET INFORMATION on behalf of a government or intelligence agency, ideally without the target realizing the intelligence was stolen. Almost anyone with access to intelligence can become a spy. But avoiding capture often takes a good cover. A cover is a fake identity that helps spies conceal their espionage activities.

Wake may have seemed like an unlikely candidate for espionage from the perspective of German officers. But like many spies, Wake used a cover based on her real identity. Her position as a wealthy and glamorous socialite concealed her espionage activities during the early days of the war. This helped her evade capture multiple times.

Most spies operate under official cover. This means a spy is posing as an official government agency employee. A spy doesn't need a high-level position to operate under an official cover. For example, a janitor or cafeteria worker in an intelligence agency's office can gather intelligence.

THE ART OF THE COVER

Spies who do not have an official cover may operate under a nonofficial cover (NOC). This is more challenging and dangerous. NOC spies infiltrate foreign governments or organizations by pretending to be someone they're not. NOC spies have no official

An NOC spy may pose as a scientist or businessperson working at a powerful foreign company.

contact with the intelligence organization they work for, giving them better access to secrets. But it also means they are on their own if caught. To stay safe, their cover must be flawless.

No matter what cover the spy adopts, they must fully commit to it. If a US spy wants a job at an Iranian nuclear facility, he or she needs to be able to speak Persian and be familiar with Iranian culture. The spy also needs a college degree in nuclear physics or engineering with a diploma as proof. And the spy will need a fake life story that is a perfect fit for the job. These details are part of the legend, or life story, for the spy's cover.

WHAT MAKES A SPY TICK?

The life of a spy is dangerous. What could make someone enter such a risky profession? Many spies, like Wake, are motivated by patriotism, or a love of their home country. Other spies may disagree with the actions of their government and choose to spy against their home country. Greed is another motivator. Foreign intelligence agencies may pay handsomely for classified information. Other spies are forced into a life of espionage through blackmail. This is when threats, such as exposing compromising information or photos, force a person to perform certain actions, such as providing intelligence.

THE LIFE OF A SPY

Spies are the most important ingredient of human intelligence (HUMINT). While some spies are volunteers, most intelligence agencies, such as the Central Intelligence Agency (CIA) or

US INTELLIGENCE SOURCES

The US government relies on five main methods to gather intelligence. These are sometimes called intelligence collection disciplines. Different government agencies lead each discipline.

OPEN SOURCE

ALL AGENCIES

Gathers information from widely available sources, such as television, radio, newspapers, online articles, research papers, and public records

HUMAN INTELLIGENCE

AGENCIES: FEDERAL BUREAU OF INVESTIGATION (FBI), DOMESTIC INTELLIGENCE; CENTRAL INTELLIGENCE AGENCY (CIA), FOREIGN INTELLIGENCE

Gathers information from human sources

MEASUREMENTS AND SIGNATURES INTELLIGENCE

AGENCY: DEFENSE INTELLIGENCE AGENCY

Gathers information from weapons and industrial activities

SIGNALS INTELLIGENCE

AGENCY: NATIONAL SECURITY AGENCY (NSA)

Gathers information from electronic transmissions, such as phone calls, satellite communications, and online correspondence

IMAGERY INTELLIGENCE

AGENCY: NATIONAL GEOSPATIAL-INTELLIGENCE AGENCY

Gathers information from photos and satellite images

An intelligence officer may spend months or years researching and building a relationship with someone before asking them to become a spy.

Federal Bureau of Investigation (FBI), recruit spies. Recruiting a spy can be delicate work, especially if the intelligence organization wants to infiltrate a highly secure location, such as a foreign intelligence agency.

Once a spy has agreed to work for an intelligence agency, they are assigned a handler. This may be the agent who recruited them or a different agent. The handler's job is to help protect the spy and collect their intelligence. The handler may also help a spy develop a cover.

FBI AND CIA

The two best-known US intelligence agencies are the FBI and the CIA. Founded in 1908, the FBI combats crime by gathering intelligence from US citizens and enforcing US laws. Founded in 1947, the CIA gathers foreign intelligence. The CIA is not allowed to gather intelligence from US citizens and cannot act on any intelligence it receives. Instead, CIA officials must share the information with government leaders or law enforcement agencies.

During the 1950s, the CIA used dead drop spikes to communicate. The handler or spy could easily push the spike into the ground, hiding it from sight.

LIFE ON THE FARM

Captured spies can face criminal charges or even execution. So, concealing activities and evading detection are some of the most important aspects of a successful espionage operation. To ensure success, CIA spies must go through a rigorous training program.

Top CIA trainees spend months undergoing classified and highly intense training on a secret military base in Virginia known as the Farm. They learn different physical and psychological techniques to stay safe, avoid detection, and become successful spies. Trainees learn to communicate without raising suspicion, known as covert communication, or COVCOM. COVCOM techniques can include signals and dead drops, where a message or package is left at a previously agreed upon location. Dead drop locations can be behind a loose brick, under a bridge, or in a hollow rock.

EVADING CAPTURE

Spies must also have skills to help them avoid and survive capture. CIA trainees learn survival skills, such as improvising weapons and treating common injuries. They also learn self-defense techniques, including weapons skills and martial arts. And trainees learn

CIA trainees also learn how to drive a boat and handle a car in a high-speed chase.

THE CHAIN OF INTELLIGENCE

A piece of intelligence gathered by a spy passes through many different hands.

SPY (AGENT, ASSET)

» Collects intelligence

HANDLER (CASE OFFICER, OPERATIONAL OFFICER)

» Recruits and manages the spy

» Plans missions

» Protects the spy's identity

» Collects intelligence from the spy

ANALYST

» Reviews intelligence gathered by spies and other sources

» Determines if the intelligence is reliable

» Consolidates the intelligence into a report

DECISION-MAKER (MILITARY LEADER, LAWMAKER, GOVERNMENT LEADER)

» Reviews the analyst's report

» Decides whether or not to act on the intelligence

techniques that help them avoid giving up information during interrogations. Psychologists study the trainees during their training to ensure they can handle the stress of being spies.

The Farm's official name is Camp Peary. It was established in 1942 to train members of the Navy Construction Battalion.

It's not known how many trainees successfully complete the elite six-month program at the Farm. But it is likely that only a fraction of recruits become field agents. And only the best agents will go on highly secretive NOC missions.

The CIA's training program is considered one of the best in the world. But spying is still a dangerous profession. And not all spies have the benefit of elite training programs to help them. Early spies relied on their wits alone to stay safe.

Ancient Egyptian clay tablets known as the Amarna Letters are one of the earliest sources to mention intelligence and espionage. The tablets date back to the 1300s BCE.

CHAPTER 3

HIDING IN PLAIN SIGHT

THE HISTORY OF ESPIONAGE IS AS LONG AS THE HISTORY OF civilization itself. Ancient Egyptian clay tablets dating back more than 3,000 years mention espionage. No one knows when the first acts of espionage actually happened, but early espionage relied entirely on HUMINT.

Many early spies used their social status to conceal their espionage activities. These spies were from social classes often ignored by people in power, such as servants and enslaved people. People from lower social classes made ideal spies because they could access and observe people in power without suspicion.

FROM ENSLAVED PERSON TO SPY

In 1781, the American Revolution was well underway. It seemed like American forces, led by General George Washington, might win the war. At the beginning of the war, the British governor of Virginia had offered freedom to any escaped enslaved person who fought for the British. And by 1781, the British needed all the help they could get.

During that time, James Armistead walked into the military headquarters of British general Lord Charles Cornwallis in Yorktown, Virginia. He informed the British officer in charge that he was an escaped enslaved person hoping to enlist and spy on the Americans for the British. As an enslaved person of a man named William Armistead, James Armistead had spent his entire life in Virginia and was familiar with the terrain and transportation routes. So, the British were pleased to have him on their side.

LOYAL TO LAFAYETTE

James Armistead's enslaved status meant Cornwallis wasn't suspicious of his offer. With the reward of freedom, it seemed natural that James Armistead would want to join the British forces.

Cornwallis ordered James Armistead to infiltrate an American army camp to spy on General Marquis de Lafayette. The assignment suited James Armistead. Earlier that year, he had agreed to spy for Lafayette. James Armistead was actually a double agent, loyal to the Patriots and Lafayette instead of to the British.

As an enslaved person, James Armistead easily moved across enemy lines, eavesdropping on conversations without suspicion. He gave Cornwallis false information about American troop numbers, locations, and military strategy. He even provided "stolen" messages written in Lafayette's handwriting.

James Armistead worked for Lafayette throughout the summer

In 1917, the Lafayette Memorial was built to honor the Marquis de Lafayette (*right*). Some historians believe James Armistead Lafayette is the second person depicted in the memorial.

of 1781, providing valuable intelligence to the Americans and misinformation to the British. In September, he passed a message to General Lafayette saying that Cornwallis was preparing to move 10,000 British troops to Yorktown. Because of this, the Americans were able to surprise the British with a full blockade. Cornwallis surrendered on October 19. This ended the war, making

James Armistead one of the most important double agents in American history. He later adopted the surname Lafayette when the general helped him obtain his freedom. He was thereafter referred to as James Armistead Lafayette.

MARY JANE RICHARDS: CIVIL WAR SPY

During the Civil War, some of the best spies used racist and sexist stereotypes to evade detection. At the time, many military officials believed Black people and women were less intelligent than white men. Because of this, military officials didn't expect them to serve as spies.

One of the most productive Union spies during the war was a Black woman named Mary Jane Richards. She worked for Elizabeth Van Lew, a wealthy socialite who ran an elaborate spy ring in

Richards is thought to have had a photographic memory. She was able to memorize the details of sensitive documents in the house of Jefferson Davis (*pictured*).

the Confederate capital of Richmond, Virginia.

As a Black servant, Richards often went unnoticed by the men around her. This made her the perfect spy! At one point, she posed as a servant looking for work at Confederate president Jefferson Davis's home. She was taken into his office by one of his staff and, while there, looked through the documents in Davis's cabinet. She then shared her intelligence with Van Lew, who reported it to Union leaders.

DOUBLE AGENTS

A double agent is a spy who pretends to spy for one government or intelligence agency while secretly spying for another. Some spies, like James Armistead Lafayette, become double agents by infiltrating an intelligence or military agency posing as a spy. Other double agents are spies who become disillusioned with their own governments. Some double agents are turned. This happens when they are captured and convinced to spy for the government they were originally spying on. Some spies even become triple agents! They work as a spy for one government while pretending to be a double agent for a different government.

THE ACTRESS SPY

The Civil War was fought entirely on US soil. Both sides shared a language, history, and culture. Many Union supporters lived in Southern territory, while many Confederate supporters lived in the North.

Cushman's acting skills aided her espionage and helped her avoid capture. She once posed as a Southern woman staying in a boardinghouse and stopped a plot to poison Union soldiers there.

As a result, some spies easily moved between territories, disguising their true intentions.

In 1863, actress Pauline Cushman was performing in Union-controlled Louisville, Kentucky, when two Confederate soldiers approached her. They offered her $350 to make a toast to Confederate president Jefferson Davis during her next performance. Not knowing what to do, Cushman asked the advice of Union Colonel Orlando Hurley Moore. He told her to accept the money, make the toast, and see him the next morning. Cushman made the toast and was fired from her acting job. But she wouldn't be unemployed for long. She visited Moore, who offered her the role of a lifetime: a Union spy.

The Confederate soldiers were impressed by Cushman's toast and thought she was loyal to the Confederacy. They invited her into their social circle, introducing her to Confederate military leaders. Cushman charmed them, learning all she could and stealing documents to pass to her Union handlers.

Cushman's acting talents helped her throughout her espionage career. She even disguised herself as a man to access places and people she couldn't as a woman. In 1863, Cushman was caught by Confederate soldiers and sentenced to death. However, she suddenly became ill, forcing her captors to delay her execution twice. Some believe Cushman's illness was an act. Either way, it saved her life! Union soldiers rescued Cushman a few days before her third scheduled execution.

Reilly infiltrated the Krupp armaments plant in Essen, Germany.

CHAPTER 4

MASTERS OF DISGUISE

In 1909, British military officials were concerned. For the last several years, the German Empire had been developing a powerful naval force with advanced weapons. Little was known about the details of the German weaponry, but the British knew it would put their country at risk. They desperately needed intelligence. Luckily, they had the perfect man in mind to gather it.

British Secret Intelligence Service officials approached Russian adventurer and spy Sidney Reilly for an undercover mission. According to Reilly, he had been working for the British foreign intelligence service, also known as MI6, for several years. In 1905, he traveled to France disguised as a priest. Once there, Reilly convinced businessman William D'Arcy to sell the rights to his newly acquired Iranian oil fields exclusively to Great Britain. This ensured Britain would have a steady supply of fuel for years to come. Now, Reilly had a new mission: to infiltrate and steal plans from a German weapons manufacturing plant.

UNDERCOVER WELDER

In preparation for his cover, Reilly learned to weld before going to Germany. He then disguised himself as a Baltic welder named Karl Hahn and started working at a German weapons plant in Essen, Germany. Reilly volunteered for the night shift, when there were fewer guards on duty, and joined the plant's fire brigade. He convinced plant managers that fire brigade members needed the full plant schematics to become familiar with the locations of entrances, exits, fire hydrants, and extinguishers. The managers agreed and allowed Reilly to study the schematics, which showed him the exact location of the office where the plans were located.

During one of his shifts, Reilly picked the office lock

Reilly was known to exaggerate and lie about his life story and achievements. So historians aren't sure how much of his story is fact or fiction.

BOND, JAMES BOND

Reilly became the inspiration for famous fictional spy James Bond. Writer Ian Fleming first introduced the character in his 1953 novel *Casino Royale*. Bond was a stylish, charming, and cool MI6 spy who had high-tech spy gadgets and was a skilled fighter. For the next decade, he appeared in multiple novels and short stories. In 1962, Bond made his first film appearance in the movie *Dr. No*. Although the character has changed with the ages, he is as beloved as ever. As of 2023, six different actors have played Bond in 26 movies, and new Bond films are still being produced.

Sean Connery was the first actor to play James Bond. He played Bond in six films between 1962 and 1971 and a seventh film in 1983.

where the plans were kept. He ended up killing a guard who caught him by surprise. Knowing others would notice the guard's absence, Reilly worked quickly. Instead of copying the plans as planned, he stole the originals, escaped the plant, and took a train to a safe house. There, he divided the plans into four parts and mailed them to British intelligence officials.

Reilly was an important asset and one of MI6's most relied-on spies throughout World War I, earning him the nickname "the Ace of Spies." His daring exploits quickly became legendary. One of Reilly's greatest assets was his ability to adopt different identities, as he did when he posed as Karl Hahn. He spoke seven languages and was an expert in changing his clothes, appearance, and accent to fit whatever role he was playing. But Reilly wasn't the only spy to rely on elaborate disguises.

Pujol was so convincing, his British handlers gave him the code name GARBO after famous actress Greta Garbo.

WORLD WAR II SPIES IN DISGUISE

In 1942, the UK domestic intelligence agency MI5 hired Spanish chicken farmer and former soldier Juan Pujol Garcia as a double agent during World War II. For the past year, Pujol had operated on his own as an independent spy, feeding misinformation to the Germans. He posed as a pro-Nazi Spanish official and German spy living in London. Pujol used guidebooks and encyclopedias to generate false intelligence reports, fooling the Germans.

After joining MI5, Pujol and his MI5 handler Tomás Harris created a fictional network of 27 spies. This network provided the Germans with a mix of false and real intelligence. Because of Pujol's efforts, the Germans missed signs of the 1944 D-Day invasion of Normandy, France, one of the war's final battles.

Pujol's disguises didn't end with the war. In 1948, he left Europe for Venezuela. He felt he could be in danger from Nazi sympathizers. So with Harris's help, Pujol faked his death. He grew a beard and wore glasses to disguise his identity. He had left his wife and children in Spain. They didn't realize he was still alive until the 1980s!

MI5 AND MI6

Like the US, Great Britain has two main intelligence organizations charged with gathering HUMINT. MI5 works to gather intelligence within the UK, as the FBI does for the US. And MI6, or the Secret Intelligence Service, functions similarly to the CIA, gathering foreign intelligence that could affect the UK's national security.

MODERN DISGUISES

Pujol used many disguise tactics similar to those intelligence agencies use. Modern intelligence agencies use advanced tools to disguise an agent's skin color, gender, hair color, or facial features with makeup and prosthetics. But more often, spies simply disguise their most obvious features. If a spy has straight hair, they might curl it. A young spy could add streaks of gray to their hair to appear older. And hair color, glasses, makeup, or a beard can quickly change the appearance of a person.

A spy's clothing should also support their disguise. Spies might change the way they walk or talk. Even the way a person stands can

A spy who is posing as a powerful diplomat might wear expensive clothing and walk with confidence.

suggest what country they are from. A spy who wants to blend in might walk with a slumped posture and wear neutral clothing. To protect their cover, spies must become talented actors who play the same role 24 hours a day, sometimes for years.

OFFICE OF TECHNICAL SERVICE

The Office of Technical Service (OTS) is a CIA department that creates modern spy gadgets. Many of the devices conceal high-tech espionage technology in everyday objects. A camera might be hidden in a pen. A coat button might contain a recording device. And a mobile phone might include lie detection software. To protect its spies, most OTS creations are classified. Very few people know what the OTS is working on!

« SPY HALL OF FAME »

JONNA MENDEZ: CIA CHIEF OF DISGUISE

In 1966, the CIA recruited Jonna Mendez and sent her on undercover missions around the world. In the late 1980s, Mendez became the CIA's chief of disguise. She oversaw the development of new disguises for the CIA's field agents. Mendez took inspiration from Hollywood filmmakers and professional makeup and prosthetic artists to learn their techniques.

Mendez with her husband. In 1991, Mendez wore a CIA mask when meeting with US president George H.W. Bush. She shocked him when she pulled it off, revealing her true appearance.

TOOLS OF THE TRADE: EVASION EDITION

DISGUISES

Spies rely on different disguises to avoid detection. A person's hair is often one of their most memorable features. One of the easiest ways for a spy to disguise their appearance is to change their hair by wearing a wig or adding a false beard or mustache. Hats and glasses can also aid the disguise.

FIVE-SECOND FACE MASK

This full-face mask could be applied without a mirror in five seconds or less. It allowed the wearer to instantly

Many disguises previously used by the CIA are on display at the International Spy Museum in Washington, DC.

transform into someone else and could change their ethnicity, gender, and facial features. Each mask was custom made to fit perfectly over the spy's real face. It took the CIA ten years to develop the technology, and when or how it was used is still classified.

GETAWAY CAR

A fast car is key to helping a spy avoid capture. This Aston Martin belonged to fictional spy James Bond and appeared in the 1964 film *Goldfinger*.

Many think the Aston Martin DB5 is one of the most iconic James Bond cars. It also appeared in the films *Thunderball*, *GoldenEye*, *Tomorrow Never Dies*, *Casino Royale*, *Skyfall*, and *Spectre*.

ESCAPE DOMINOES

During World War II, British intelligence agencies hid escape maps inside sets of dominoes. The maps helped prisoners of war and pilots who had been shot down behind enemy lines.

Dominoes like these were used by Britain's World War II military intelligence unit MI9. The dominoes contained sections of a map of Burma.

Boyce (*center*) hid in a drainage hole for three hours before escaping the Federal Correctional Institution in Lompoc.

CHAPTER 5

ESCAPE ARTISTS

ON JANUARY 21, 1980, CHRISTOPHER BOYCE ESCAPED FROM the Federal Correctional Institution in Lompoc, California, where he was serving a sentence for espionage. Using a makeshift ladder and a pair of tin snips, Boyce cut a hole in the barbed wire fence surrounding the prison and slipped through. By the time prison guards performed their 10:00 p.m. bed checks, Boyce was long gone.

Boyce had started working at the classified communications center of California aerospace agency TRW in 1974. As part of his job, he had a security clearance and access to highly classified US satellite technology information.

In 1975, Boyce began selling these secrets to the Union of Soviet Socialist Republics (USSR), or Soviet Union. He recruited his childhood friend, Andrew Daulton Lee, to deliver copies of the documents on microfilm to the Soviet embassy in Mexico. Boyce and Lee made $76,000 for their espionage activities. But in 1977, Mexican authorities arrested Lee, who confessed to his and Boyce's espionage. Boyce was arrested, and both men were sent to prison.

FINDING THE FALCON

Boyce's 1980 escape triggered a global search by the FBI and US marshals. Despite their efforts, Boyce seemed to have disappeared into thin air. To avoid capture, he spent the first few weeks after his escape hiding in the wilderness near Lompoc. As a skilled outdoorsman, he survived by eating insects and wild berries. When the search died down in central California, Boyce made his way to the Pacific Northwest, eventually settling in Bonners Ferry, Idaho.

Boyce was nicknamed "the Falcon" and Lee "the Snowman." The 1985 film *The Falcon and the Snowman* (*pictured*) was based on their exploits.

Boyce adopted the name Jim Namcheck and spent his first few months in Idaho camping in the wilderness, only traveling into town to get supplies. He eventually moved to a safe house for fugitives run by a woman named Gloria White. To make money while living with White, Boyce began robbing banks. With the help of various disguises, including a fake beard, he robbed 16 banks in the area, stealing more than $30,000.

In July 1981, Boyce moved to Port Angeles, Washington, under the name Sean Hennessey. He seemed to be tired of hiding and had an active social life. But his freedom was nearly up. On August 21, a team of US marshals and FBI agents, acting on a tip from one of Boyce's Bonners Ferry contacts, surrounded a car in a small Port Angeles restaurant parking lot. They arrested Boyce, who was in the front seat, and sent him back to prison.

SAFE HOUSES

Safe houses are locations where spies or criminals can hide from law enforcement or others who are looking for them. A sympathetic friend or family member of a spy might run a safe house. Other safe houses are purchased and run by intelligence agencies. Safe houses can be used for offensive or defensive purposes. An offensive safe house provides a safe place for spies to plan and execute covert operations. A defensive safe house is a safe and protected place for a spy to hide from capture or surveillance.

SPIES EVERYWHERE

Boyce's espionage took place during what is often considered the golden age of espionage: the Cold War. This was a period of conflict in which the US and its allies competed with the USSR and its allies for technological and military superiority. The countries never openly fought during this time. Instead, they waged secret battles using information to keep their rivals from gaining too much power.

The intelligence industry thrived during the Cold War, with hundreds of thousands of

During the Cold War, intelligence agencies hid bugs in clothing and accessories. CIA agents could record conversations using bugs hidden in jewelry, pins, or buttons.

spies working to gather state secrets. Countries around the world established and grew huge intelligence agencies to manage their espionage activity. For the USSR, it was the KGB and GRU. For Britain, it was MI6. And the US had the FBI and the CIA.

During this time, intelligence agencies often relied on listening devices known as bugs. These devices typically only contained a radio transmitter and a microphone. This simplicity meant a bug could be unbelievably small and hidden in anything. Bugs became a powerful tool for counterespionage, including spy hunting. But no tool is quite as powerful as a spy hunter's gut feeling.

BECOMING AN AGENT

Getting a job at the CIA or FBI is a sure way to find yourself on the front lines of covert intelligence. To become a CIA or FBI agent, you must be a US citizen with a college degree. It helps to speak more than one language. Aspiring agents need to complete a lengthy application process and pass a background check. They also need to pass medical and fitness requirements before beginning a rigorous training program.

In 2012, Sandy Grimes coauthored *Circle of Treason: A CIA Account of Traitor Aldrich Ames and the Men He Betrayed*, a book about her experience and hunt for Ames.

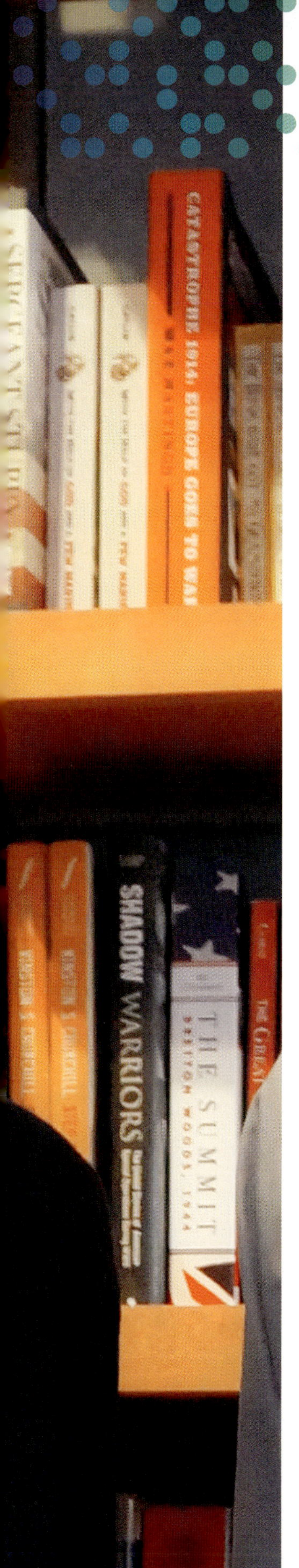

CHAPTER 6

HUNTING SPIES

In 1991, after two decades as a CIA officer, Sandy Grimes was ready to retire. Although relatively young, she was satisfied with her career and wanted to spend more time with her family. But before Grimes could officially put in her notice, the CIA's counterintelligence chief approached her. He needed Grimes for one last job.

Over the last six years, the CIA had lost more than 30 double agents who had been spying on the USSR. The Soviets had captured and executed many of these agents. CIA officials believed one of their own was a mole who betrayed them. Whoever the mole was, they had access to highly classified information and until they were caught, no CIA spy was safe.

Grimes was more than willing to join the hunt, code-named Operation Playactor. She had been a handler for a spy the Soviets captured and executed in 1985. No one knew who had outed the spy, but Grimes was eager to bring them to justice. And she already had a prime suspect: her colleague and former friend Aldrich Ames.

TO CATCH A SPY

Grimes had known Ames since her early days in the CIA. They had even carpooled to work together for a while. Grimes remembered Ames as a sloppy dresser who was disorganized and always ran late. But ever since he had returned from a CIA post in Rome, Italy, she had noticed a change in her friend. Now, Ames drove a fancy car, wore expensive suits and shoes, and had an air of self-confidence and arrogance he had never shown before. Grimes knew Ames could not afford this lifestyle on his CIA salary and suspected he was working for the KGB. But that wasn't enough to arrest Ames.

Grimes and the small Operation Playactor team made a list of every CIA officer who had access to the lost agents' identities.

The CIA's Operation Playactor team consisted of (*clockwise from bottom left*) Grimes, Paul Redmond, Jeanne Vertefeuille, Diana Worthen, and Dan Payne.

The team narrowed the list to 28 suspects. After interviewing each suspect, they narrowed the list down to the top three suspects. Ames was at the top.

Grimes began investigating Ames. She watched his every move, reviewed all his CIA work, and studied his friends, family, and professional contacts. She noted when he came into the office each day, ate lunch, and clocked out. Soon, Grimes compiled a timeline of Ames's life and daily activities. Meanwhile, she had also been tracking Ames's financial activities. She noticed a series of suspicious financial deposits after Ames had met with a Soviet diplomat suspected of working for the KGB. This was the proof Grimes needed.

Operation Playactor turned this information over to the FBI, who began surveilling Ames. To arrest him, they needed to catch Ames in an act of espionage. The FBI bugged Ames's phone and office and searched his trash. They even assigned an agent to work as Ames's assistant and report on his activities. On February 21, 1994, FBI agents arrested Ames. He was tried and sentenced to life in prison for espionage. Grimes retired from the CIA soon after his arrest, her work finished.

COUNTERINTELLIGENCE

Hunting spies is part of an agency's counterintelligence effort. In the world of espionage, counterintelligence is just as important as intelligence. It includes activities designed to mislead the enemy, prevent espionage, and protect national secrets. An intelligence agency's counterintelligence department also works to discover and catch spies. The department may also give false information to a spy known to be an enemy.

Most captured spies are discovered by rival intelligence organizations. Other spies may betray them, but sometimes spies get careless and reveal themselves, or blow their cover. One of the most common ways spies blow their cover is by changing their behaviors. For example, a spy who typically goes to bed early might decide to take a late-night walk, attracting attention.

Intelligence agencies use different tactics to find spies. When Operation Playactor was hunting Ames, the CIA manually reviewed the case files of all the suspected moles. The FBI also set up an elaborate system of bugs and surveillance devices to track Ames's every move. These tactics worked, but they took years of research and observation. With the rise of modern technology, spies now have a new tool to help evade detection: the internet.

The FBI arrested Ames outside of his home in Arlington, Virginia.

« SPY HALL OF FAME »

ALDRICH AMES

As the CIA's chief of intelligence for the Soviet division, Aldrich Ames knew all about the KGB and how it worked. He made many Soviet contacts, recruited spies for the US, and even unmasked enemy spies.

But Ames needed money and knew intelligence could make him a wealthy man. In 1985, Ames walked into the Soviet embassy in Washington, DC. He gave the KGB the names of double agents who were spying for the US. For the next nine years, Ames provided intelligence to his Soviet handlers.

The Soviets paid Ames more than $2.7 million for his information, the largest amount of money they ever paid an American spy.

In 2013, US president Barack Obama created a panel to investigate the government's surveillance practices because of Snowden's actions.

CHAPTER 7

DIGITAL EVASION

On June 7, 2013, an explosive report hit newspapers and media organizations around the world. A whistleblower had provided a top-secret document showing that the National Security Agency (NSA) had been gathering intelligence from the servers of US internet service providers (ISPs) since 2007. The operation, code-named PRISM, allowed the NSA to access all the digital activity of its targets, including emails, video calls, social media posts, and even websites that a target visited. But PRISM wasn't just spying on the military or intelligence officials typically targeted by intelligence agencies. PRISM also spied on average US citizens.

A few days later, Edward Snowden came forward as the whistleblower. He worked for the NSA as an information technology security expert but came to believe the agency's digital surveillance tactics were unethical. Although he tried to raise his concerns with his superiors, nothing changed. Snowden decided the only

THE ESPIONAGE ACT OF 1917

The Espionage Act was enacted in 1917, shortly after the US entered World War I. It prohibited anyone from stealing, copying, photographing, or recording information related to national defense with the intent to harm the US. People who violated the act could face fines, prison, or even execution if the espionage crime was considered serious enough.

The US charged Snowden under the Espionage Act of 1917. To avoid arrest, Snowden fled to Moscow, Russia, where he was granted asylum and later Russian citizenship.

course of action was to release what the NSA was doing to the world.

Snowden's revelations made him a controversial figure. Some hailed him as a hero who was protecting their privacy and right to free speech. But to US intelligence agencies, Snowden was a traitor and a spy. Hero or traitor, Snowden's actions pulled back the curtain on an aspect of spying many never considered: cyber espionage.

CYBER ESPIONAGE

Cyber espionage is the practice of using technology to gain access to intelligence such as military or political secrets. Cyber espionage can help organizations, such as governments or militaries, gather information about their enemies, assess possible threats, sabotage their enemies, and even prevent possible attacks. Officially, no country admits to engaging in cyber espionage. However, many countries secretly back groups of cyber hackers to spy on their behalf.

Normally, a person's internet activity is tracked by their ISP. The ISP can share the information with a third party, such as an advertiser or intelligence agency.

Today, cyber security and espionage are some of the most important aspects of intelligence gathering and counterespionage. The FBI is the primary US government agency that investigates and prevents cybercrimes, including cyber espionage. Its cybersecurity experts protect US intelligence using many of the same tools that hackers use. Because of this, cyber espionage often becomes a game of cat and mouse between hackers and the cybersecurity experts searching for them.

HIDING OUT ONLINE

Many cyber spies conceal their activities on the deep web. This is where more than 90 percent of online content exists. Standard search engines, such as Google, cannot access this content. Many of these websites require a user to log in or otherwise restrict access.

Spies who manage to evade detection often fade into history. And the best spies often receive little or no credit for the risks they take.

Others block search engine crawlers, or bots, that find and index internet content for search engines.

Most information on the deep web is innocent. One example is information on a bank website that requires a username and password to access. However, about 5 percent of all internet content is on the dark web, which is part of the deep web. Dark web content is only accessible with a specialized browser, such as the Onion Router (TOR). TOR sends internet traffic through a series of random servers, making it nearly impossible to track a user's online

The rise of social media has made posing as a different person easier than ever. Modern spies can develop a fake social media profile online in a matter of minutes.

CYBER HYGIENE

Cyber spies can be anywhere and everywhere. The best way to beat cyber spies is to practice cyber hygiene. These practices can help keep you safe and protect your information online. Here are some simple ways to protect your information:

» When using public Wi-Fi, only visit encrypted websites. This means the website scrambles data into a code. Look for a lock symbol on the left side of your web browser search bar to know if a website is encrypted.

» Do an app cleanup. Uninstall any unused or duplicate apps.

» Keep all devices and applications fully updated at all times.

» Change your passwords frequently. Don't repeat passwords across websites. Make sure your passwords don't contain any personal information that could be easily guessed.

movements. And since no one regulates the dark web, it hosts a lot of illegal activity. Many cyber spies and terrorists use the dark web to plan their attacks.

Spying, whether online or in person, can be a lonely and dangerous profession. The risks are high, and captured spies face arrest, exile, or even execution. But this doesn't stop spies and spy hunters as they do their best to make the world a better place.

SO YOU WANT TO BE A SPY?

Spies can be anywhere and everywhere. Your favorite aunt, swim coach, or school principal could be a spy! Almost anyone can become a spy. But being a spy who can evade capture isn't easy. Do you have what it takes to create a cover? Complete the missions below to find out!

MISSION 1
ENCRYPT AN ESCAPE MAP

WHAT YOU NEED

pencil

paper

Choose the area you want to map out. It could be your home, school, neighborhood, or somewhere else. Make a sketch of the area on a sheet of paper, including an escape route to help you leave the area. Now, encrypt your map. Create symbols that stand for different places on your map. A classroom could be a heart and hallways could be vines or flowers. On a fresh sheet of paper, copy the map using only the symbols. Make sure to destroy the original!

MISSION 2
DESIGN A DISGUISE

Spy disguises don't always involve elaborate costumes, wigs, or fake glasses. In fact, some of the best disguises involve making small changes to the way you look and act. Walk across the room in front of a mirror. Pay attention to details about your appearance, such as your posture, stride, and facial expressions. Now, repeat the walk, but this time, make small changes to each detail. If you stood up straight, try slumping your soldiers. If you were smiling, try frowning. You could even try the spy trick of putting a pebble in your shoe to create a limp!

MISSION 3
CREATE A COVER STORY

Spies working undercover are often forced to deceive the people closest to them. Can you create a cover story convincing enough to fool your friends and family? Come up with three stories about something you did last weekend. Two stories should be the truth and include real details. The third should be fictional but believable. Tell the three stories to someone who knows you well, such as a family member or close friend. Can they spot the lie?

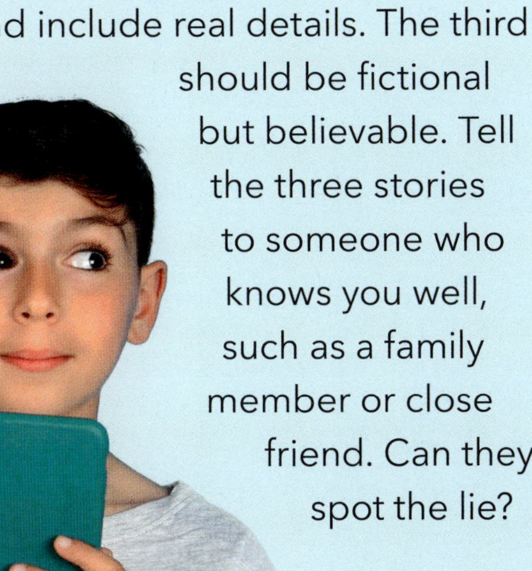

TIMELINE

The American Revolutionary War
1775–1783

1781
James Armistead begins spying on British general Lord Cornwallis.

The American Civil War
1861–1865

Actress Pauline Cushman begins spying for the Union.
1863

1864
Mary Jane Richards begins spying for the Union.

1909
Spy Sidney Reilly infiltrates a German weapons manufacturing plant and steals plans.

World War I
1914–1918

World War II
1939–1945

England forms the SOE, employing female spies.
1940

1942
Juan Pujol Garcia becomes a double agent for British intelligence agency MI6.

1943
Nancy Wake escapes Nazi guards in France and joins the SOE.

1947–1991
The Cold War

1980
Christopher Boyce escapes from prison, where he is serving a sentence for espionage.

1985
Aldrich Ames begins spying for the KGB.

1991
CIA agent Sandy Grimes joins Operation Playactor to find Soviet mole Aldrich Ames.

1994
Ames is arrested and charged with espionage.

2013
NSA worker Edward Snowden leaks a report showing the NSA has been spying on people's online activity.

GLOSSARY

blockade—the cutting off of an area by soldiers or ships. A blockade prevents supplies and people from going into or out of an area.

brigade—a group of people who are put together to do a special task.

checkpoint—a point at which an inspection or investigation is performed.

Civil War—the war between the United States of America and the Confederate States of America from 1861 to 1865.

classified—kept from the public in order to protect national security.

COVCOM—covert communication. Covert communication is the secret exchange of information or data.

eavesdrop—to secretly listen to a private conversation.

espionage—the secret gathering of information on others.

ethnicity—the relation to a group of people based on a common race, nationality, religion, or culture.

evade—to get away from or avoid by skill or trickery.

gender—the behaviors, characteristics, and qualities most often associated with either the male or female sex.

guerrilla warfare—fighting that uses sudden, small, surprise attacks against enemies. A guerrilla is a person, usually a member of an independent unit, who uses guerrilla warfare.

hacker—a person who illegally accesses a computer system.

infiltrate—to enter a place secretly and without permission.

microfilm—reduced-scale photographs of a document or other printed material on a film.

mole—a spy who establishes a long-term cover within an organization.

patriotism—love of and devotion to one's country.

prosthetic—of, relating to, or being an artificial device that replaces a part of the body.

sabotage—to harm an enemy nation's defenses by damaging or destroying something on purpose. A saboteur is someone who sabotages an enemy nation.

schematic—a drawing or diagram of a plan, or a map.

sexist—related to the unfair treatment of people because of their sex.

socialite—someone who is well-known and social among wealthy people.

state secret—piece of information kept secret by the government.

stereotype—a widely held but overly simple idea about a group.

surveillance—close observation of someone or something.

whistleblower—someone who reports secret information about illegal or problematic activity.

ONLINE RESOURCES

To learn more about spy evasion, please visit **abdobooklinks.com** or scan this QR code. These links are routinely monitored and updated to provide the most current information available.

INDEX